C000129715

Poems of the Point

Lauri Cruver Cherian

A Publication of The Poetry Box®

Poems ©2022 Lauri Cruver Cherian
All rights reserved.

Editing & Book Design: Shawn Aveningo Sanders
Cover Design & Photo Editing: Robert R. Sanders
Cover Photos Provided by Lauri Cruver Cherian
Author Photo by Kari Cruver Medina

No part of this book may be reproduced in any manner
whatsoever without permission from the author, except
in the case of brief quotations embodied in critical essays,
reviews and articles.

ISBN: 978-1-9+56285-23-9
Printed in the United States of America.
Wholesale Distribution via Ingram.

Published by The Poetry Box®, October 2022
Portland, Oregon
ThePoetryBox.com

For my parents, Roy and Corinne,
who purchased a piece of beach waterfront in 1957,
made life on the Point possible,
and filled our home with music, love and kindness.

❧

Special thanks to my siblings, Kari and Kyle
for half of a century of beach fun and simpatico.

Contents

"Everything is better at the beach. Even rain."

—Author Unknown

Coming Home

I am not home until I see
the Tacoma Narrows Bridges
looming dark against the sky,
suspended securely,
reaching across the strait
connecting Tacoma to Gig Harbor.

I am not home until I see
Anderson's store to the right
and Point Fosdick to the left.
Memories of childhood bike rides
and adventures awarded
with a 20-cent Snickers bar.

I am not home until I see
Mrs. Lewison's farm overgrown and wild.
Memories of visits all in Norwegian.
Her wrinkled ruddy face
and long faded blonde braid
wound 'round her head like a Norse crown.

I am not home until I see
forests dense with fir and pine
pointing to the cloud-filled sky.
Pt. Fosdick leading me up-hill and down
around a corner until finally
the dead end is in sight.

And I am home.
The bay greets me with sparkling winks,
enticing me to turn down the last steep hill
past the white name signs
with fewer familiar and more unfamiliar names
until I see my own father's name.

[. . .]

And the memories wash over me...
Unraked autumn leaves crunching underfoot.
Sprinting up the hill breathless to catch the morning school bus.
Freshly plucked Italian plums tucked in my pocket.
A wrinkled brown lunch bag clutched in my hand.
Walking my best friend home up the hill to the dead end
because playtime was long over.

Magical snowy winter days and school closures.
Black bouncy inner tubes swooshing down the snow-covered hill.
Fruit trees exploding in spring blossoms.
Fragrant knockout roses lining the driveway.
Summer-ripe red raspberries and blackberry bushes.

Waves lapping at barnacle encrusted beach rocks.
Rain drizzling on welcoming leaves.
Sea air filling my hungry lungs,
my heart and mind with childhood happiness,
love, peace, and contentment
that have lasted half a century
when I come home.

Pt. Fosdick

Sun kissed sand
Immersed toes
Scent of salt and seaweed
Waves advancing and retreating
Rhythmic, hypnotic, peaceful
Light dancing across the surface of the deep blue bay
Lazy clouds lingering overhead
Calls of the seagulls breaking the peace with their demands
Hums of motor boats replacing the gulls
Slapping the waves as they race past
Birch leaves rustling in an unexpected breeze
Caressing my cheek
Welcoming me back home to Pt. Fosdick

The Bay

Waves roll and tumble
Playful hellos
And teasing goodbyes
Invite me to sit
On smooth gray wave polished stones
Pick one up
And toss it in... *ker plop*!
Gilded concentric circles ripple
Shimmering on the water
Rugged purple peaks
Of the Olympic Mountains
Home of the gods
Hold up the falling golden sun
As it retires
Sending orange ribbons
To trail across the sky

Boat Ride

The speed boat smells of
SEA & SKI, seaweed, and kelp.
We sit strapped in child-sized orange life jackets
stiff with age and salt water
wide-brimmed hats cockeyed on our heads
and a picnic basket at our feet.

Dad pushes off wetting one shoe in the effort.
One hard paddle and he's cleared the rocks.
Hush! Hold your breath, will the motor start?
The motor is let down.
A key is turned…Vroom VROOM, it started!
Relief. We are off!

The bow hits the waves spanking our bottoms.
We grip our hats and the side of the boat
Sea water spritzes our faces.
Gulls chase and cry overhead.
Snow covered Mt. Rainier appears on cue to say
"I'm here!" on this July day.

Around the corner from Fox Island
in the Carr Inlet awaits "Dead Man's Island."
We reach the shore of the uninhabited island
spilling out onto welcoming sand
picnic basket, shovels, and buckets in hand
ready to dig for clams.

Under the Weeping Willow

Under the weeping willow
drip long green leaves
lazily stroking the mossy grass
cut by my grandfather's wooden hand-push lawn mower.

Blades spin "Clip, clip, clip!"
Grass flies up in green confetti clouds
filling the air with the familiar sweet scent
and musical sounds of summer.

Four long fishing poles
lay discarded on the grass.
Gentle bursts of fresh sea air
tickle and play with the leaves overhead.

Three little siblings huddle
next to their Daddy kneeling in the grass
staring wide eyed at two large black eyes
staring back…dead but watchful.

Awaiting their fate
on a wooden cutting board.
A sharpened knife
poised to slice open the pale fleshy stomachs

of two brown speckled Pacific codfish.
Auburn scales glistening in the sun.
Three little voices gasp, "AH!"
as Daddy's knife slices through the soft underbellies.

Entrails spill out gruesomely.
Six green eyes squeeze shut,
then squint open afraid to miss
the horrible contents of the fish.

A knife is offered to whomever
wants to pop the air sacks
like bursting birthday balloons.
My brother stabs twice, "Pop! Pop!"

"EW!" The delighted chorus sings
as curious seagulls fill the air
demanding one to another, "Come and see!"
hoping to benefit from the fishing trip.

The tide accompanies
with its rhythmic song
like a steady drum.
It's summer under the weeping willow.

The Kitchen

Embers crackled and popped
dancing fiery red.
Heat spread across our backs
like warm hugs.

We snuggled,
three siblings shoulder to shoulder
pajama bottoms on the long stone slab hearth
in front of the rustic brick fireplace.

Wide smiles on young faces,
listening to the clear voice of Julie Andrews
singing about the hills
and a few of her favorite things.

Our stocking feet swinging like a metronome,
hands cupped around dishes
of vanilla ice cream and Ovaltine,
while rain tapped friendly hellos on the rooftop.

The fireplace lays cold now.
A chilly gust escapes through the flue.
The stone hearth is bare
but the rustic bricks still stand.

Holding together the memories
of joyous laughter, music, and song.
The love that once permeated the kitchen
will fill it again.

We Danced in Your Light

You delighted in motherhood
Your magic and zest for life
shone like bursts of fireworks
unable to be contained

We danced in your light
blossomed in your love
took baby steps and then great leaps
because of your encouragement

As you watched
As you cheered
As you beamed your bright light
Then we left

You carried on
finding other ways to light the world
alone but never lost
in the darkness of loneliness

Your rays found others
to encourage
to uplift
to illuminate

Until your time was sufficient on earth
You left
but like a firefly's flash
and a fairy sprite's glow

Small playful explosions in the darkness
remind us
it will be alright
Joy, laughter, and light will return

The Garage

A whistle floats out the garage door
and trips along on the breeze
under the cherry tree
over the smooth gray beach rocks

I catch the notes
It's a show tune of course
I name it and sing it back
You hear and we share a smile

The garage smells of paint and sawdust
It smells of you
So much time spent building and mending
making things better for those you love

Big worn hands discolored from the day's projects
A finger bound with a BAND-AID
from a hammer that missed its mark
I peek through the door and you are there

The garage remains as you left it
waiting to be of use
I step inside and breathe
take in your essence

Allow you to fill my heart
again, with your music
Tunes never forgotten
whistled in the garage

Bing Cherries

The metal bucket clangs
against the rough trunk of the cherry tree
I shinny high up into the branches
over the garage rooftop
peering through foliage
for dark purple Bings
hanging in plump
heart-shaped pairs
waiting to be noticed
winking at me in the sun
I reach out and pluck them

Cradled in the boughs
I devour them until my belly protests
Blood red juice drips from my chin
Pits rain down on unsuspecting heads
Bings drop into the bucket with a *plunk, plunk*
It fills too quickly
I'll have to ease my way down
careful not to lose a precious pair
Life is good on this summer day
After all, it's just a bowl of cherries

Picking Raspberries

I had very few chores as a child.
In fact, if I practiced the piano for thirty minutes,
I got out of dish duty altogether.
But one summer chore
I couldn't evade
was picking raspberries.

I'd work my way to the back of the fence,
trying not to think of what might be under
the thick prickly bushes
keeping an eye out
for that fat black rat
that frequented the compost heap.

Looking for the ripest raspberries
plucking them nimbly
keeping the berries intact.
Others would be ripe by tomorrow,
making it necessary to come back again
to pick bowl after bowl of raspberries.

Mom would make freezer jam
for our Saturday morning pancakes.
And I complained…
What I would give
to travel back in time
and gladly pick the raspberries.

Morning on the Bay

The coffee cup warms
my chilled fingers
A blanket hugs my shoulders
as the sun wakes over the bay

Ready for breakfast
the eagle soars and drops
dive bombing
into the misty gray depths

Surfacing with a silver salmon
tight in its talons
returning to perch
at the top of a tall pine

Herring balls disturb the water
popping like rain drops
attracting flocks of seagulls
breaking the morning peace

A silver spotted harbor seal
like a playful pup
submerges to chase breakfast
reappearing to watch me watch him

Sunset over the Olympics

A
rainbow sunset
drips pastel
over royal blue peaks
of the Olympic Mountains
Rock toes cool along the shore
in the pale green of Wollochet Bay
curtained by outstretched arms
of dark black pines

Orcas

Great black sails rise from the deep
slicing through the water.
We spy you rounding the corner
from the Narrows into Hale Passage.

Neighbors sprint from their houses
congregating along the shore
eager to catch a glimpse of
Southern Resident Orcas.

J Pod on a hunting mission
swimming, breeching, spy hopping.
They are the Yin and Yang
of the deep.

Legend says that Orcas protect
those who travel away from home
and will lead them back when the time comes.
I hope it's true, and they lead me back to the Point.

Where the Eagle Lives

She wanted to take me down the beach
where the eagle lives on Point Fosdick
overlooking the Tacoma Narrows Bridges.
She visits him often.

So proud to show me,
she points to his perch
high up on a madrone branch
overhanging the beach.

She giggles
because there he is.
Isn't he wonderful?
He's waiting for her.

Sitting statuesque
watching us below
as we observe him above.
I will remember the spot.

I should have known
by the bleached bones of fish
and assorted mammals discarded in the sand below
a little graveyard of beach creatures.

I will remember next time
to look for you
when she is gone.
She will be pleased

That each time
I walk down the beach to the Point
I find you
and I find her again.

Moon Snails

We used to find moon snails,
Lewis' Moon Snails,
smooth, white, and round
like a small breast.
It's rare to find a perfect whole moon snail.

The moon snail lays her eggs in a collar of sand
scattered at low tide.
Millions of tiny eggs mix with sand grains
forming a perfect shirt collar.
Eggs later hatch and swim away.

We'd gather them
wear them around our necks,
discarding them
to dry in the sun,
oblivious to their importance on the beach.

I've found only two perfect moon snails.
One I gave away with a piece of my heart
to a sweet sixteen first love.
I wonder if he still has it
and thinks fondly of me?

The second I hold dearer
for it reminds me
of my love for my daddy
who used to enjoy walking the beach
searching for moon snails.

Sand Dollars

Low tide
Race to the sand flats
Squishy and cold
Beneath summer calloused feet
Exposing sand bubbles
Seaweed and starfish
Upturning rocks
That hold promise
Of families of crabs scattering
Their sanctuary disturbed
Searching for sand dollars
Buried treasure
Burrowed beneath the sand
Gray discs stamped
With a five petaled poinsettia
Five small white doves in flight
Hidden inside
Symbol of peace and goodwill
A generous offering
From the Puget Sound

Bullwhip Kelp

Long brown bullwhips
crack and snap
biting at bare ankles
Whips not made
of genuine cow leather
but of bullwhip kelp
Nereocystis
"mermaid's bladder"
washed ashore
broken off
from a floating canopy
Bulbous top
like a seaweed light bulb
Ten-foot rope
gripping rocks
on the floor of the bay
Kelp forests breathing
like the ocean's lungs
buoyant and dancing
with the pull of the tide
providing a food web
supporting rockfish, salmon, and orca
Haven for playful sea otters
Beach fun for young siblings

Jellyfish

It's the dog days of summer
Transparent jellyfish
drift and pulsate
like bubbles through the waves

We catch them and
hold them in the palms of our hands
lopping them at each other
Get hit and you're out!

Cross-legged we balance
on homemade wooden paddle boards
Paddling over the kelp canopy
deeper into the bay

We wonder what creatures lurk beneath us
Then we see it … a Lion's Mane jellyfish
Like red and orange Jell-O
but with stinging tentacles trailing two feet behind

Hold still and let it pass
We have no desire to share the bay
with this jellyfish
traveling lazily with the current

Pacific Geoduck

You are really

quite alarming

Panopea Generosa

Long

Soft

Fleshy

Encased

in a huge white clam shell

Great effort is taken

to chase you down

deep into the sand

scoop you up

and laugh

at what you resemble

Growing Up with Music

Our love affair with music
began with *Tura Lura Lura,*
an Irish lullaby sung bedside
by our tender-hearted father

Whispered goodnights and sleep tights
bedtime concerts sung by siblings
in three-part harmony
You Are My Sunshine and *Mockingbird Hill*

Burl Ives singing about a *Little White Duck Swimming in the Water*
Soundtracks to *The Sound of Music, Winnie the Pooh,* and *Jungle Book*
The Mills brothers crooning *Basin Street Blues*
Herb Alpert's and the Tijuana Brass with *Whipped Cream and Other*
*   Delights*

Dueling pianos played competing composers
Beethoven, Bach, Haydn, and Chopin
Compositions penciled at the grand piano
Performed in the living room

Eight track tapes inserted during car trips to the Oregon Coast
The Carpenters and John Denver
serenading us on summer vacations
We were *On Top of the World*
until *Country Roads* took us all the way home

Father's calloused fingers strumming on the guitar
They Call it That Good 'Ole Mountain Dew and *Red River Valley*
Blazing beachside campfires
Big Dipper spilling out stars overhead

Bee Gees, Earth, Wind & Fire, and the Doobie Brothers
jostling for control of the airwaves, *Minute by Minute*
as Puccini's haunting melodies pulled our heart strings from PBS
Growing up with music

Birthdays by the Bay

Under the shade of the weeping willow
neighborhood friends gathered.
Laughter mixed with the crash of waves
Mom sat center stage, scissors poised over a bag of marshmallows.
What will she cut from a single marshmallow,
a bunny, a squirrel, or an elephant?

☍

Restless pirates pillaged the beach
"Ahoy Matey, we be diggin' for pirate plunder!"
Black Jolly Roger flags
Skull and cross bones
marked the spot
as each boy dug up his buried pirate booty

☍

Little girls in homemade kimonos
graced the beach
like delicate cherry blossoms
dancing under the overhanging madrone boughs
Sipping tea and eating cupcakes
at a bayside Japanese tea party

Bayside Sushi

The tea serviced is set
on the long sun-bleached log
It's a bayside sushi bar
with a scenic view of Fox Island

A young tow-headed chef
prepares the fresh seaweed
carefully chosen at the bay's edge
seasoned with sand and sun-dried crab parts

Little hands carefully roll it up tight
A dull kitchen knife left to rust in the sand
saws small slices of sand and crab shell sushi
Ready for the taking, sushi anyone?

The Singer Hummed

The Singer hummed
throughout the night
Christmas Eves, birthdays,
and autumn's new school year

The steady surge of the pedal rocked us to sleep
as we dreamed of treasures
wrapped in tissue paper
ready by dawn's light

Pooh Bear would have a new nightshirt
matching sleeping bag and pillow
For Barbie and her entourage, new wardrobes
Sisters had matching wrap-around skirts

Stiches were expertly executed
lasting half a century
carefully preserved
awaiting a third generation's play

Back to school trips to the fabric store
thumbing through Butterick and McCall's
Playing hide and seek in a maze of fabric bolts
with groovy florals and bohemian paisleys

Spinning the display of notions
around and around
Matching thread to fabric
buttons, lace, ribbons, and rickrack

Then it happened, as it always did
The dreaded conversation
with a stranger or a friend; it didn't matter
It meant a long wait sandwiched between aisles of fabric

[. . .]

Naughty me
stepping on Mommy's toes
signaling my patience had run out
an hour ago

Ready for that promised stop at Baskin-Robbins
for a single scoop of Jamoca almond fudge
then home to hold the Butterick pattern in my hands
imagining I was that stylish girl on the cover

Mom measured, pinned, and cut
working magic like a shoemaker's elf
not by the light of the moon
but by the light of the humming Singer

Junk from the Dump

The Chevy wagon returned laden with junk from the dump
A shop teacher's supply house of treasures
Iron pipes, scrap metal, bicycle parts
Truck inner tubes and tires

Miraculous transformations occurred in the garage
Like Santa's busy workshop
We heard the tap tap tap of a hammer
The buzzing of a circular saw and rattling of a spray paint can

Bikes appeared on birthdays
Iron teeter totters spun in the yard
Innertubes complimented turning bars
And floated lazily on the tide

Tire swings hung from an accommodating willow tree
Tetherball stand stood ready
For neighborhood competition
Childhood amusements crafted with junk from the dump

The Fourth of July

We never knew if the 4th would bring
Rain or shine in the Pacific Northwest
But it certainly brought the company of good friends
Hotdogs, pre-boiled in a pot at Mom's insistence
Mrs. O's red wine vinegar potato salad
Charred marshmallows warranting
Mom's annual cautionary tale of carcinogens
Sticky s'mores with two extra Hershey's squares
Inserted when no one was looking
Homemade blackberry pie á la mode
Sour cream cheesecake topped with fresh raspberries
No need to choose just one dessert
When the paper plate accommodates two
Fireworks competing on both sides of the bay
Like a field of battle between Fox Island and Gig Harbor
A roaring, spitting, hungry bonfire devouring the wood offerings
Smoke following the most beautiful
Dad strumming the guitar like Roy Rogers on the Texas trail
A celebration of country, family, and friendship

The Beach Hasn't Changed

The beach hasn't changed
Does it know you are gone?
That only your spirit hovers silently over the rocks?

You strolled down the beach over crushed seashells
joyously accompanied by three little dachshunds
tails wagging and bottoms shimmying

Your eyes scanned the bay
for large dark doglike heads
and ample behinds of sea lions diving for salmon

You bent and picked up smooth flat rocks
skipped a rock or two...one, two, three, four, five times
and felt like a kid again

You waved to the old neighbors
still inhabiting their original beach cottages
and new neighbors in houses too large rebuilt on the beach

No, the beach hasn't changed
The glassy surface still holds
unseen secrets deep below the drop-off

Heavy barnacle covered stones when upturned
still hold a place for crabs, periwinkles, and limpets to hide
The heron stands motionless at the shore

The eagle waits on the madrone
turning his head ever so slowly
Maybe he is looking for you

As I do, walking down the beach
in quiet reflection
accompanied by your spirit

Once

Once
The Narrows Bridge stood sentinel
Guarding the coast on the strait of Puget Sound
Strong, pale green, and solitary
Cable lines pulled taut in suspension
The meeting of two sides
Welcome, beckon, and bid farewell

Once
A century before, canoes paddled
Puyallup and Nisqually tribes
Through the strait to Fox Island
An internment camp hastily erected
Tribes herded into reservations
No choice, no respect
Their present and future stolen
Then forgotten

Once
Ferry boats carried passengers
From Tacoma to Gig Harbor
Blowing their whistles
Three long blasts of salute
Until roads and bridges were built
Whistles long forgotten

Once
Fishing vessels and ferry boats
Were built in the harbor
Fishing nets mended
In the net sheds by the bay

Once
The Galloping Gertie danced
In forty-two mile per hour winds
Oscillating and crashing
Swallowed by spinning currents in the Narrows
Built stronger and better
With lessons recorded
In engineering history books

Once
Yarns were spun of enormous octopuses
Lurking in the depths below
Mt Rainier "Tahoma" hiding
Shrouded in a cloak of clouds
Olympic Mountains framing the bay
In purples and blues

Now
A pair side by side
One green, one gray
Stand together and share the space
The past and the present
Twins spanning the strait
Too many cars and too many retirees

Once
My home

Wiener Dogs

Sun's warm touch
Heats red velvet coats
Of three little wiener dogs
Spread out on Daddy's lap
Like a blanket
Napping together on the chaise lounge
Bayside on a lazy afternoon
The day's to-do list set aside
A snuggle and a cuddle
Is what's needed now
For the moment
Each one glorying in their repose

Touchstones

Caress of a cool sea breeze
leaving goosebumps on my skin
Waves drumming a sea shanty on the shore

Circling gulls
awaiting handouts
Sun glittering gold on the bay

Mt Rainier
an apparition
behind the Tacoma Narrows Bridges

Seaweed and clam shells
left abandoned
by the receding tide

Plop, plop, plop
of King Salmon at dusk
Watercolor sunset melting over the Olympics

Campfire songs
strummed in the key of C
Voices blended in three-part harmony

Tunes carried
across the bay to Fox Island
as the bonfire spits and crackles

Seven stars
of the Big Dipper
winking in the night sky

Dad's toothy smile
Mom's spontaneous laughter
Sunday afternoon calls with small talk and weather updates

[. . .]

Reminders to stay positive
Take your vitamins
Concluding with I love you and I'm so proud of you

These
are my touchstones
My home on the Point

Love Has Lived Here

Love has lived here
In the calloused hands
That built this house
On a patch of perfect beachfront property
Carried heavy wooden beams
Laid rustic fireplace bricks
Built and stained golden cabinets
Shoveled wheelbarrows full of sand
Hauled beach rocks
Sowed seeds and tended a garden
Carved names on growing pumpkins
Potted flowers and moved them to a sunny spot
Planted apple, plum, and cherry trees
Raised three children
Bought two pianos
Paid for voice, dance, and piano lessons
Filled the house with music
And left a legacy
Love has lived here on the Point

Praise for Poems of the Point

I've long wanted to visit places in the Northwest like Gig Harbor, Washington. Now, via Lauri Cherian's beautiful poems, I can. *Poems of the Point* is brimming with beautiful descriptions of a special place and great truths about the power of family, loyalties and traditions. When Lauri tells me in the first poem how certain landmarks and memories bring her home to Gig Harbor it brings me home as well, to the very distant and different little East Texas town that raised me many years ago. Lauri is a gifted poet and storyteller; I will come back to this collection occasionally.

—Ron Rozelle, author of *Into That Good Night*,
The Windows of Heaven and *Touching Winter*

Poems of the Point recaptures a delicious childhood of bike rides, beach walks, and twenty-five-cent Snickers bars. Cherian's strong images recreate the salty shores of Puget Sound, transporting the reader to places washed by memory and love. This debut collection is a heartfelt tribute to the enduring power of place.

—Susan Donnelly, poet and teacher

This is a paean—not just to a place, but to moments. Lauri Cherian's poems are present—to nature, to family, to love. Her arresting verses call us to pay attention to beauty, both material and invisible. Her writing transports us to her childhood home and beckons us in. Lauri Cherian's work calls to mind Annie Dillard; full of keen observations and making meaning out of memory.

—Sneha Abraham Villalva
Executive Speechwriter, UCLA

[...]

Lauri Cherian's collection, *Poems of the Point,* invites us to wander barefoot in the cool sands of childhood memories and family tributes. Rich in detail, from gutting Pacific Codfish (*A knife is offered to whomever/ wants to pop the air sacks*) to searching for moon snails (*... lays her eggs in a collar of sand*), Cherian's poems describe a deep attachment to home. In "Orcas" we learn: *Legend says that Orcas protect/ those who travel away from home/ and will lead them back when the time comes.* Cherian's poems are a delight-filled homing journey to Gig Harbor.

—Ann Farley, author of *Tell Her Yes*

About the Author

Lauri Cruver Cherian is a Washington State native raised in Gig Harbor on a beautiful piece of beachfront property. She awoke each morning to the cry of the seagulls and the view of the bay in her front yard, which was glorious in rain or shine. Her childhood memories are rich with singing around the bonfire, boat trips with her dad, fishing and clam digging, paddle boarding in Wollochet Bay, and watching for sea lions and orcas that would often swim past her house.

Lauri has lived on the South Texas Coast for three decades. She holds a Master's degree in Language Acquisition Education from the University of Houston and a Bachelor's degree in Bilingual Education from Washington State University. Lauri has taught English as a Second Language for children and adults for twenty-five years and is a teacher trainer, consultant, and a workshop leader in adult ESL. She is the recipient of several teacher of the year awards including District Bilingual Teacher of the Year in Spring Branch Independent School District in Houston. (You can visit her website at https://lessonswithlauri.com for more information.)

Besides returning to the beach when she gets the chance, Lauri enjoys acting in community theater, singing, and playing the piano, traveling, and writing short stories and poetry. Her poem "Courage" dedicated to healthcare workers during the pandemic, won honorable mention in the Texas Mental Health Creative Arts Contest in 2021. Lauri and her husband have three adventuresome adult children.

laclauriloo@gmail.com • facebook.com/lauri.cherian

About The Poetry Box®

The Poetry Box, a boutique publishing company in Portland, Oregon, provides a platform for both established and emerging poets to share their words with the world through beautiful printed books and chapbooks.

Feel free to visit the online bookstore (thePoetryBox.com), where you'll find more titles including:

What We Bring Home by Susan Coultrap-McQuin

In the Jaguar's House by Debbie Hall

Shells in the Seive by Nathan Fryback

The Weight of Clouds by Cathy Cain

Let's Hear It For the Horses by Tricia Knoll

Of the Forest by Linda Ferguson

Songs from Back-in-the-Back by Marcia B. Loughran

The Catalog of Small Contentments by Carolyn Martin

Tell Her Yes by Ann Farley

Moroccan Holiday by Lauren Tivey

A Nest in the Heart by Vivienne Popperl

Late Fall Bucolics by Anne Coray

This Is the Lightness by Rachel Barton

Earthwork by Kristin Berger

Fencelines by Angela Hansen

and more . . .

Lightning Source UK Ltd.
Milton Keynes UK
UKHW021038060223
416538UK00017B/2424

9 781956 285239